Your Will, LORD Not Mine

*Discovering God's
Plan for Your Life*

by Benny Hinn

Your Will, LORD Not Mine
by Benny Hinn

Scripture taken from the King James Version of *The Holy Bible*

Your Will, LORD Not Mine
©2003 Benny Hinn Ministries

ISBN 1-59024-171-1

CONTENTS

INTRODUCTION

Howbeit when he, the Spirit of truth, is come,
he will guide you into all truth: for he shall not
speak of himself; but whatsoever he shall hear,
that shall he speak: and he will shew you
things to come. (John 16:13)

QUAN [1]

Quan's family immigrated to the United States from Southeast Asia when he was only five years old. For many years, before and after the move, Quan remembers hearing his parents talking about America as "the land of opportunity." And he watched as they made it so.

Quan watched initially as both of his parents worked eighteen-hour days doing sweaty, back-breaking jobs no one else wanted. Within five years, the family had its own small business. Quan and his siblings were expected to help, before and after school, as well as during vacations. Within ten years, the family owned several businesses. During the ensuing years, Quan graduated from a prestigious university and then went on to earn his MBA from an equally well-known business school. Quan now runs the family empire, which has grown to several states.

"My parents taught me well," Quan shares. "I am a product of the proverbial American Dream. Our family is living proof that you can truly become anything you want to be in this wonderful country, if you are willing to work tirelessly and dream big. I've tried to teach my children the same principles of self-determination.

---

[1] Quan, Betty, Mary, and Sam are composites of real people, used in this book for illustration purpose only. Fictitious names have been used, and certain details changed, to protect privacy.

"But I often wonder what I'm missing. I have all the 'things' that anyone could want, yet I still feel empty inside sometimes. Maybe I just expect too much of myself. Probably the emptiness I feel, at times, is what keeps propelling me forward to make things better for my family and my employees. Maybe it's just something I have to learn to live with. What do you think? Am I expecting too much? Is there something wrong with me?"

BETTY

Betty's eyes burn with fierce determination as she tells her story. "Even back to the time when I was a child," she begins without hesitation, "I have lived with one main motto: I'm going to do what I want to do, when and how I want to do it.

"I remember looking at my mom, defiantly, and telling her that I couldn't wait to grow up so I could get out on my own and do whatever I wanted. That represented freedom and happiness for me. My mom was a Christian, and she always said Dr. James Dobson should have put me on the cover of one of his books, *The Strong-Willed Child*. It's true! I just always had it in me to make it on my own, to do whatever I wanted. It was as if I was just born to be that way."

Betty thinks for a moment and then continues: "You want to know the funniest part? I'm forty years old, serving at least five more years in this prison before I can hope for parole, and I'm surrounded by eight hundred other women, most of whom still talk about getting out so they can do what they want to do, when they want to do it—the exact thing that got them locked up here in the first place."

She looks around at her surroundings, then says, "Ironically, for several years after I came here, I still believed that nobody was going to tell me what to do. This place is filled with people still acting tough and defiant. Well, I finally wised up to the fact that I was being told exactly what to do every moment of my life, even while I kept believing the exact opposite. When I finally figured that out, and what was wrong with ME-ME-ME, it was the beginning of seeing a real change. I'm taking classes, going to chapel, and finally starting to do something worthwhile with my life."

MARY

Mary's smile is known to millions. She flashes it often as she talks, as if offering an easily recognized signature. Her gestures and voice inflections are perfectly timed, as if she is following a script.

"I became a Christian when I was at the top," Mary shares. "I wasn't a miserable failure like so many come-to-Jesus stories I hear. I did it because it just made sense. I wanted to do the right thing and make sure I went to heaven in case anything ever happened to me.

"Since then, it's as if everything has gone wrong. I'm still successful, but it's just not as satisfying as before. It's as if the bottom has dropped out of my life. My husband and I fight more than ever. I've had run-ins with people I've always gotten along with. I don't feel comfortable doing a lot of the things I used to do, and that makes me wonder if I'm going to be perceived as a Jesus Freak or something, and if that will affect my career.

"And even my time with the Lord is weird—when it once seemed so fresh and new a few months ago, now it sometimes feels as if my prayers are bouncing off the ceiling. Sometimes this whole Christian life is so confusing. I used to think I had all the answers, and now I wonder if I know anything at all about serving Jesus. What's wrong with me?"

SAM

"I teach at a Christian college," fifty-something-year-old Sam starts. "I pastored a number of churches before I started teaching here, and I still fill the pulpit whenever I'm needed. Few people here know all of the details of my life. They see me as a nice, funny guy with a wonderful wife. They know I have grown kids who live in another state. What they don't see is all the heartache I caused."

He looks to see if his comment causes surprise, then continues: "I was the golden boy of my denomination from the time I was in college. I was student body president, preached in some of the best churches while I was still in seminary, did the right things, said the proper things, and looked the part. By the time I was thirty, I had it all—one of the finest churches, my picture in the church periodicals, a place at the head table during national conferences."

Sam clears his throat as if searching for the proper words to explain. "But," he adds, "I lost it all by forgetting that pesky little verse about pride coming before the fall. That, and the part about doing God's will, not my will. It took losing nearly everything before I finally figured out that doing God's will doesn't mean doing whatever I want and belatedly asking His blessing on my decisions.

"If there's anything I want to teach my students, it's the fact that God isn't in the business of making us self-satisfied, self-centered, and self-serving. No! His desire is for us to be molded into His image, no matter what it costs.

CAN YOU KNOW GOD'S WILL?

Lots of questions arise when the conversation moves to the subject of God's will:

- How can I know for sure I'm doing what I'm supposed

to be doing with my life?

- I've messed up so much—how can I get back on track?

- I really want to serve God and do His will, but how do you really know if you're doing His will?

- Can you really know what His will is?

- I've heard people talk about God's perfect will and His permissive will. What's the difference?

Let me say this without any reservation: **God loves you and has a plan for your life!** In fact, knowing that you're living in God's perfect will is the most exciting life you can experience. You see God at work in your life. You get to enjoy the blessings that follow. You get to touch other people with a life-giving message.

But when you're living outside God's perfect will, life can be a dead-end. Wrong decisions made outside God's will not only affect you but may affect your family members and their future.

People often know, deep inside, that a master plan exists for their lives. Some call it destiny. Others call it providence. Many simply call it fate. Christians know (or should know) that this master plan is God's perfect will.

I'm more convinced than ever, from studying God's Word and reading about the lives of great men and women, that God wants to speak to and share His will with each of us. Go back and reread the John 16:13 passage that begins this book. This Scripture tells us three things about the Holy Spirit:

1. **The Holy Spirit guides us into all truth.** If we are sensitive to the leading of the Holy Spirit, He

will use the Word of God to help us make the right decisions as we seek His will.

2. **The Holy Spirit speaks to us on behalf of God.** If you are a Christian, the Holy Spirit is already speaking to you. The more you listen and obey, the better you hear Him.

3. **The Holy Spirit shows us things to come.** When we make decisions, the Holy Spirit can reveal future events that may affect or be affected by that decision.

As a Christian, you already have the Holy Spirit at work in your life, guiding you into all truth, speaking on behalf of God, and showing you things to come. My hope is that this book will help you to better understand the work of the Holy Spirit in your life.

SEEKING HIS WILL

Every Christian should seek to know God's will. God spoke to the prophet Jeremiah:

> Then the word of the Lord came unto me, saying, Before I formed thee in the belly I knew thee; and before thou camest forth out of the womb I sanctified thee, and I ordained thee a prophet unto the nations. (Jer. 1:4-5)

Even before Jeremiah was born, God had a plan for his life. He formed Jeremiah with the purpose of making him a prophet to the nations. In the same way, God has a plan for your life. He may not be calling you to be a prophet to the nations, but you have no less of a calling on your life. It is your responsibility to find God's plan for your life.

And while it's true that God has a blueprint for you, it's also true that the devil has a plan for your life. Jesus very clearly pointed out the difference between His will and the devil's:

> The thief cometh not, but for to steal, and to kill, and to destroy: I am come that they might have life, and that they might have it more abundantly. (John 10:10)

Throughout life, we face two roads that we can follow—God's road of abundance and life—or Satan's road of destruction and death. It's that clear-cut, the overload of mixed messages thrown at us notwithstanding. The choices we make determine whether or not we will experience God's blessing or not.

My prayer is that you will choose the way of God's perfect will and experience the riches of His blessings throughout all of your life.

Chapter 1

YOUR WILL, LORD

Wherefore be ye not unwise, but understanding
what the will of the Lord is. (Eph. 5:17)

God has a wonderful plan for your life. This plan is
directly connected to His perfect will. Discovering
His perfect will comes about progressively as we
learn to hear God's voice.

Whether you need to make a decision concerning a job
opening, a potential spouse, a ministry opportunity, or your
child's education, I've got good news for you. All of us face
crucial decisions, and God cares about all of them, even the
small ones. Jesus said:

> Wherefore, if God so clothe the grass of the
> field, which to day is, and to morrow is cast
> into the oven, shall he not much more clothe
> you. (Matt. 6:30)

God not only cares about the decisions you make, He
wants you to make decisions that reflect His will for your life.
Ephesians 5:17, quoted above, commands us to know God's will.
To know His will is to be wise. Not to know God's will is to be
unwise and ultimately devastating.

Let's explore specific ways to hear God's voice concerning His will for your life. In this chapter, however, let's take first things first.

Here are three foundational truths concerning God's will:

Principle #1: You cannot find God's will apart from the Lord Jesus.

1 Thessalonians 5:18 declares, "In every thing give thanks: for this is the will of God in Christ Jesus concerning you." You cannot, in other words, know God's will apart from Christ Jesus.

Anytime I communicate with people through books, crusades, broadcasts, or one-on-one, I realize that people come from a variety of backgrounds. Perhaps you have been a dedicated Christian longer than I've been alive. Others—perhaps you— have never heard the Gospel before and are desperately seeking answers for questions you thought you'd never be asking.

Here's a basic starting point for everyone, regardless of background, education, or culture. The first step toward knowing God's will for your life is to make sure that you have Jesus living in your heart.

If you haven't done so already, is there any good reason why you cannot receive Jesus Christ into your heart right now? If you are willing to let go of your burdens and challenges, and if you will repent of your sins and recognize Jesus Christ as your Lord and Savior, you can accept Him at this very moment.

At this moment, you can pray the most important prayer of your life. You can use words such as these:

> Lord Jesus, I've tried to make it by myself, but I need You to help me. I know that I'm a sinner. I realize that I need Your forgiveness. I believe that

9

You died for my sins. I want to know Your will for my life, and I now invite You to come into my heart and my life. I trade my worst for Your best. I trust You as my Savior. I want to follow You and live for You. I pray this in Your precious name. Amen!

If you prayed that prayer and meant it, the Bible has more life-changing promises for you than you could ever imagine. They include, foremost, the one found in Romans 10:13: "For whosoever shall call upon the name of the Lord shall be saved."

The Bible offers this truth as well:

> Therefore if any man be in Christ, he is a new creature: old things are passed away; behold, all things are become new. (2 Cor. 5:17)

When you receive Christ into your heart, you join a special family—the family of God. You begin your life in Jesus Christ. And the journey you are starting is an exciting one as you discover God's plan for your life and live it out each day, starting today.

Principle #2: God's will is always good.

If it's not good, it's not God! Although bad things can happen to good people in the natural, in the spiritual realm God's will is always good. The Bible is clear on this subject:

> And be not conformed to this world: but be ye transformed by the renewing of your mind, that ye may prove what is that good, and acceptable, and perfect, will of God. (Rom. 12:2)

When God is involved, you can be in the midst of a problem and still have total peace. You can be going through a storm yet remain calm. If there is any evil presence or demonic oppression, it's not good and it's not God. If there's no peace, there's no God.

Principle #3: God's will must be sought.

Understanding God's will involves a transformation ("be ye transformed"). The word transformed in the Greek language is where we get the word metamorphose, as in when a caterpillar becomes a butterfly. All of us have seen beautiful, colorful butterflies that bear little, if any, resemblance to the larvae they once were.

Understanding and doing God's will means that you will go through a total transformation throughout your life. First, you present your body to God. Then, you allow Him to transform your mind. Understand that if your body does not belong to God, your mind cannot be renewed. So, your body and mind must both belong to God.

You and I will not discover God's will unless we search for it. God's will becomes clearer to us as we mature in the ways of the Spirit. The more we read the Word and spend time in prayer seeking God's will, the more God responds.

Jesus said, "My sheep hear my voice" (John 10:27). Just as sheep recognize the voice of the shepherd, true believers are attuned to the voice of God. The longer you are a Christian, the more accustomed you are to the ways of God. A heightened knowledge of the Word and a growing familiarity with God's voice enables you to more readily recognize God's leading.

GOD'S WILL

God's will for you is good, acceptable, and perfect.

When you discern God's will, you find goodness, acceptability, and perfection before God.

Goodness will surround you. The minute you are in the will of God, you will find goodness everywhere you go. Everything you do has the potential to prosper. Everything you touch is blessed. There is goodness, goodness, goodness. This doesn't mean you won't have any challenges—far from it. But you will have a peace that will guide you through those problems.

You will be acceptable before God. The Bible tells us that through Jesus Christ, God "hath made us accepted in the beloved" (Eph. 1:6). When you become a Christian, your life is hidden in Christ, and you receive eternal life.

God's answer will be perfect. The word perfect means "complete." God doesn't stop halfway through a project and then quit. His desire is to transform you into His image.

God will reveal His will to you. As you obey Him, follow in the steps He has set before you and allow Him to transform you. You will learn to hear His voice, and as you learn to listen to His direction more and more you enter into the most exciting life possible to mankind.

Chapter 2

HEARING GOD'S VOICE

The voice of the Lord is powerful; the voice of
the Lord is full of majesty. (Ps. 29:4)

God speaks to us in a number of ways, each distinct
and different. Regardless, though, how God chooses
to speak to us, everything He says and does is in
response to our prayers.

When we call upon Him in prayer, He may choose to
respond in any way He chooses. Here are seven of the most
common ways He reveals His will.

God's Voice #1: His Word

And in the first year of Darius the son of
Ahasuerus, of the seed of the Medes, which
was made king over the realm of the
Chaldeans; in the first year of his reign I Daniel
understood by books the number of the years,
whereof the word of the Lord came to
Jeremiah the prophet. (Dan. 9:1–2)

Daniel makes clear in this passage that the avenue
through which God most often speaks to us is His Word. Daniel
tells us that he "understood by books," in this case through his
reading of Jeremiah. That's how the brave man of God knew
what God's will was for his life.

The Bible is God's written Word, and God uses it to speak to us as we read. I have read the Bible cover to cover many, many times. During each reading I discover new meanings in even the most familiar passages of Scripture. As God allows me to see words or teachings in a whole new light, He speaks to me about a specific matter for which I am seeking His direction.

It's always such a wonderful surprise to read something I've read many times before. It's as if a light goes on! A familiar passage seems to leap off the sacred pages of my Bible and burn itself into the depths of my being. On many of these occasions, God has used Scripture to provide specific answers to my questions about His will.

God's Voice #2: Dreams and Visions

At times, God speaks to His children through visions and dreams:

> And it came to pass, that, when I was come again to Jerusalem, even while I prayed in the temple, I was in a trance. (Acts 22:17)

The apostle Paul related an especially remarkable and history-changing vision of Jesus:

> And saw him saying unto me, Make haste, and get thee quickly out of Jerusalem: for they will not receive thy testimony concerning me. And I said, Lord, they know that I imprisoned and beat in every synagogue them that believed on thee. (Acts 22:18–19)

Paul's plan was to stay in Jerusalem and preach to those who knew Him. He had made up his mind on what to do for God. Yet in a vision from God Paul learns that his plan is not God's plan for his life. Paul had his own plan for his life, and

God changed it through a vision. As a well-known Pharisee, Paul may have thought that his profile among the Jews would allow him to use his influence to persuade them to follow Jesus and that this, surely, would please God.

This was not God's will, and only as Paul prayed for direction was God's guidance revealed. Knowing that the Jews would not receive Paul's message, God spoke to Paul in a vision and told him that He was sending Paul among the Gentiles. Paul's life was changed because of God's visionary response to Paul's prayers and obedience. As a result, the Gospel was preached throughout the known world.

God's Voice #3: Circumstances

Circumstances can be very tricky. Some people go through life, bouncing from one stumbling stone to the next, blaming God for everything that happens to them. It doesn't take too much discernment to realize that Satan loves to trip believers anyway he can, then blame the Lord for what happens. People fall for this ruse all the time.

On the other hand, God sometimes speaks through circumstances because the answers are difficult to miss. Circumstances can be excellent ways in which God chooses to show His direction. There are many examples throughout the Bible. One of my favorites is when Abraham's servant Aleazar prayed that God would lead him in the matter of choosing a wife for Isaac:

> And he said O Lord God of my master
> Abraham, I pray thee, send me good speed this
> day, and shew kindness on my master
> Abraham. Behold, I stand here by the well of
> water; and the daughters of the men of the city
> come out to draw water: and let it come to
> pass, that the damsel to whom I shall say, Let

down thy pitcher, I pray thee, that I may drink; and she shall say, Drink, and I will give thy camels drink also: let the same be she that thou hast appointed for thy servant Isaac. (Gen. 24:12–14)

We are told that Aleazar asked God to have the appropriate choice fulfill certain conditions. By having a woman fulfill those conditions for Aleazar, God used circumstances to convey His will to Aleazar regarding Isaac's future wife.

Another excellent story of circumstances is Gideon and his fleece (Judges 6). Gideon asked for specific circumstances to make sure God was really directing him into battle against the Midianites. God moved specifically. God could have chosen to direct Gideon through some other manner, but in this case He answered through very specific circumstances.

God's Voice #4: Prophecy and the Gifts of the Spirit
The apostle Paul was a mighty man of God, yet it's recorded in Acts 21:10 that the Lord sent Agabus to speak to Paul through prophecy, thereby confirming something that the apostle already knew deep in his heart.

Today, some individuals are so desperate to hear from God that they go from place to place in search of a "word from God." I believe that God speaks through prophecy at times, but I am convinced that we must be very careful. The best place to get direction regarding God's will for your life is with a Bible open or in your prayer closet. Get to know the Lord, and you will hear from Him and get to know what He is saying to you.

In the end, prophecy is intended for three specific purposes: "Be he that prophesieth speaketh unto men to edification, and exhortation, and comfort" (1 Cor. 14:3). Edification means building you up in faith. Exhortation encourages you to move forward. Comfort reassures and calms.

A prophetic word should confirm what you already know deep down in your heart. Above all, it must agree with Scripture.

God's Voice #5: An Audible Voice

Occasionally, God speaks to His children through an audible voice. The Scriptures record that God spoke audibly to and, indeed, face-to-face (mouth to mouth) with Moses:

> Hear now my words: If there be a prophet among you, I the Lord will make myself known unto him in a vision, and will speak unto him in a dream. My servant Moses is not so, who is faithful in all mine house. With him will I speak mouth to mouth. (Num. 12:6–8)

When God called me to serve Him, I was a teenager planning to study hotel management at Seneca College in Toronto, Canada. I had already paid for my first semester's classes. Just before I was to start, I was waiting on a city bus when I suddenly heard a voice saying, "Go home!"

At first I thought my mind was playing tricks on me. The bus came. People boarded it. Then the vehicle sped up the street. It was as if I was frozen to the spot.

"Go home!"

I thought, "This is mad. It can't be!"

Again, a third time the voice came: "Go home!" So I went back home, totally bewildered. My mom asked, "Back so soon?"

I told her I wasn't going to college.

"Not going?" she shot back. "What do you mean, not going?"

17

"I don't know," was the only reply I could say. Can you imagine what my mom thought? I didn't even know what to think. I knew that I had heard an audible voice.

A week after I heard that voice, Jim Poynter, a Free Methodist minister, asked me to go with him on a charter bus trip to Pittsburgh. The group was going to a healing meeting with evangelist and Bible teacher Kathryn Kuhlman. I didn't know much about her, but I didn't want to disappoint Jim. How my life was changed because of that trip! God touched my life profoundly at the meeting.

I didn't get on the city bus because I heard His voice, yet I'm so grateful I stepped onto the charter bus a week later as it headed to Pittsburgh. His next steps were revealed to me there. Never in my life had I been so touched by what I experienced that day. Soon afterward I received the Holy Spirit's baptism, and an entirely new world opened up for me.

God's Voice #6: Similitudes
Sometimes, God speaks through a likeness or image (what in Hebrew is known as t'mnuah) so powerful you cannot get it out of your mind:

> I have also spoken by the prophets, and I have
> multiplied visions, and used similitudes, by the
> ministry of the prophets (Hos. 12:10)

The first time this happened to me was on the day that I was born again. I was sitting in history class, my favorite subject in school. That day, however, history took second place. I had just received my wonderful Lord Jesus at ten minutes before eight that morning, and my heart was overflowing with love for my Savior. As I sat in class, I suddenly saw an image of myself wearing a suit and preaching before a massive crowd. I didn't understand what I saw. At that time, I didn't own a suit and certainly couldn't speak well.

God gave me a similitude or image of my future that morning in 1972. And everything that I have done from that time to today has confirmed what once was merely an image.

Whenever I stand before the thousands in miracle crusades around the world, I'm reminded of the picture I saw in my mind that morning in history class. God has been faithful in accomplishing His will in my life, and I see the fruits in every miracle crusade!

God's Voice #7: Supernatural Peace

God's peace always resides where He is. Therefore, when there is no peace, it's a good possibility that you are heading the wrong way:

> And the peace of God, which passeth all understanding, shall keep your hearts and minds through Christ Jesus. (Phil. 4:7)

The late William Barclay, a world-renowned Bible commentator and minister with the Church of Scotland, made the following profound observation regarding God's peace:

> It may be that one of our great faults in prayer is that we talk too much and listen too little. When prayer is at its highest we wait in silence for God's voice to us; we linger in His presence for His peace and His power to flow over us and around us; we lean back in His everlasting arms and feel the serenity of perfect security in Him.

I have learned from personal experience that this kind of perfect peace is an important key to discerning God's will. When my heart is filled with an indescribable peace that surpasses all human understanding, I am in the center of God's will.

The wonderful minister and writer R. A. Torrey wrote this simple-yet-profound statement:

> The only man who is at all competent to interpret the will of God is the man who is in harmony with God, and the only man who is in harmony with God is the man whose will is fully surrendered to God.

Throughout Scripture we read of a loving God who seeks to communicate with His people. His purpose for creating us, in fact, was to enjoy a close relationship with us. He wants us to follow the Lord's example, Jesus said, "My meat [purpose] is to do the will of him that sent me, and to finish his work" (John 4:34).

To be in the will of God, we must be willing to obey Him and do His will.

Chapter 3

DOING GOD'S WILL

Now the God of peace, that brought again
from the dead our Lord Jesus, that great shepherd of the sheep, through the blood of the
everlasting covenant, make you perfect in
every good word to do his will, working in you
that which is wellpleasing in his sight, through
Jesus Christ; to whom be glory for ever and
ever. Amen (Heb. 13:20–21)

Jesus described people who are not spiritually discerning as
those who "seeing see not; and hearing they hear not, nei-
ther do they understand" (Matt. 13:13). Some people heard
Jesus preach and understood His message of the Kingdom, but
others heard Jesus preach and never understood. This was true
even among His disciples.

God guides His people today in the same way. Some people recognize God's voice and understand, but others fail to recognize God's voice and therefore are unable to discern His
direction. Even among His modern-day disciples is this true.
They have eyes but do not see and ears but do not hear.

FOUR STUMBLING BLOCKS

Knowing God's will must include the development of spiritual "eyes" to recognize God's direction in your life. Begin by understanding the four stumbling blocks that can detour or stop you from knowing and doing God's will:

Stumbling Block #1: Living in Sin

When King David confessed his sin with Bathsheba to God, he prayed, "Make me to hear joy and gladness" (Ps. 51:8). Before, he had been living in sin, but now he prayed to the Lord to ask forgiveness for his sin and to be made able to hear God's voice again.

The nature of sin is that it creates a barrier between God and us, as the prophet Isaiah described: "But your iniquities have separated between you and your God" (Isa. 59:2). Sin will cause your ears to get plugged so that you cannot hear God's voice.

Granted, I'm not saying that any of us, except Jesus, lives perfectly and without sin. What I am referring to is the willful practice of sin that we already know is wrong. If you are struggling with gluttony, change your eating habits. If you are engaged in an unholy relationship with a person of the opposite sex, confess your sin and quit doing what you are doing.

Stumbling Block #2: Hatred and Bitterness

Although this could also be considered living in sin, it deserves separate mention. Here is how people who struggle with hatred and bitterness are described in 1 John 2:9-11:

> He that saith he is in the light, and hateth his brother, is in darkness even until now. He that loveth his brother abideth in the light, and there is none occasion of stumbling in him. But he that hateth his brother is in darkness, and walketh in darkness, and knoweth not whither he goeth, because that darkness hath blinded his eyes.

Hatred and bitterness will keep you from knowing God's will. In fact, when you have a problem understanding God's will in your life, it's always a good idea to examine your life to see if you hate or are embittered against someone. If you are, ask the Holy Spirit to give you the strength to forgive, the sooner the better!

Stumbling Block #3: Busy-ness

We live in a busy society. Everything today is rush, rush, rush. We rush to work. We rush home. We rush to church. And we attempt to rush God into showing us His will, right now!

God simply doesn't live according to our timetables and the ways of this world. We yell, "Now, Lord!" He says, "Be still, and know that I am God" (Ps. 46:10). You simply cannot know God and His will until you are still enough to listen. In Psalm 23:2 we read, "He leadeth me beside the still waters."

The apostle Paul wrote in 2 Corinthians 11:3:

But I fear, lest by any means, as the serpent beguiled Eve through his subtilty, so your minds should be corrupted from the simplicity that is in Christ.

God isn't in a rush just because we choose to be. In fact, we know that God is not the author of confusion but of peace (1 Cor. 14:33).

Stumbling Block #4: A Made-up Mind

George Müller (1805–1898) was a Prussian-born English evangelist and philanthropist. A man of faith and prayer, he established numerous orphanages in England. Once, he was asked, "How do you find God's will?" and he replied, "When you come to God, have no mind in the matter. Come to God without your mind made up."

It's good advice, today, more than ever. When we seek God's direction with our minds already made up, we usually hear only what we want to hear. And if God answers differently than we expect, we assume that He hasn't answered us.

We must be on-guard against these four stumbling blocks. If you allow sin into your life, you will miss God's will. If you allow hate and bitterness to control you, you will miss God's will. If you allow busy-ness and confusion to set in, you will miss God's will. If you seek God with your mind already made up, you will miss God's will.

Always be ready to confess and to turn from your sin. Forgive those who have hurt you. Wait on God. Seek God with no will of your own: "Your will, Lord, not mine!" It requires an awesome act of faith to set your will aside.

FOUR STEPPING STONES

Just as there are four major stumbling blocks to knowing God's will, there are four vital stepping stones that are helpful in getting you to where you can hear God's voice:

Stepping Stone #1: Humility

After confessing to God his sin with Bathseba, King David prayed: "The sacrifices of God are a broken spirit: a broken and a contrite heart, O God, thou wilt not despise" (Ps. 51:17).

If you want to know God's will for your life, make sure you have a humble heart. God will find you unacceptable if you are clothed with pride and arrogance.

Too often Christians arrogantly make demands upon God and then wonder why He doesn't guide them. Ironically, I've found that when you come to Him in true humility, God will move heaven and earth to speak to you and direct your paths.

Stepping Stone #2: Reverence

"O fear the Lord, ye his saints: for there is no want to them that fear him," wrote King David (Ps. 34:9). Fearing God does not mean being scared of Him; it means reverencing Him. We come boldly before the throne, yet we do so with respect. He is the Creator of everything. He is God Almighty.

When we approach Him, not only must we come with humility, but we must also come to Him in reverence. I'm more convinced today than ever that people who fear God lack nothing, including direction from God.

Stepping Stone #3: Maturity

Doing God's will means understanding the process of maturing in the Lord. We must never be content to remain babies in Christ:

> For when for the time ye ought to be teachers, ye have need that one teach you again which be the first principles of the oracles of God; and are become such as have need of milk, and not of strong meat. For every one that useth milk is unskilful in the word of righteousness: for he is a babe. But strong meat belongeth to them that are of full age, even those who by reason of use have their senses exercised to discern both good and evil. (Heb. 5:12–14)

We cannot know God's will, nor can we mature as Christians if we lack knowledge of God's Word. That's as simple as it gets.

We must feed on the Word, memorize it, meditate on it, pray over it, and apply it to our lives. Otherwise, we will remain infants, never recognizing God's voice or His will. It's part of getting to know the Lord personally. We can't, however, expect maturity to happen overnight, for it is a process.

In many trades, a beginner is called an apprentice. Apprentices must be instructed because they are unskilled. They make mistakes, so their supervisors must check their work. However, as they commit themselves to learning their trade they mature into journeyman, a competent and skilled tradesman.

Unfortunately, many Christians remain throughout their lives as nothing more than apprentices—mere babes in Christ—because they have no experience of knowing God, His ways and His Word. They are still infants. This is a tragedy that is all too common.

You cannot know the will of God unless there is growth in your life spiritually. There is no such thing as standing still. Change is constant in the Kingdom of God. You are either developing daily into the image of Jesus or reverting to carnality.

Growth is vital. If you are not growing and progressing in the things of the Spirit, you will experience difficulty recognizing God's voice.

To every born-again believer, God gives a measure of faith (Rom. 12:3). Through exercising that faith in God—knowing God, His word and His ways—the Christian becomes increasingly able to understand what is God's will. Anything less is a catastrophe!

Stepping Stone #4: Prayer
If you want to know God's will for your life, you must use what God plants in you at salvation. The second you are born again, the Holy Ghost deposits a seed within your life that gives you the ability to hear God's voice. That seed is watered through prayer.

You will never know God's will without watering this seed every day. If the seed is watered sporadically, its growth will be stunted. This seed must be watered every day because God speaks daily. In John 15:7, we are told, "If ye abide in me, and my words abide in you, ye shall ask what ye will, and it shall be done unto you."

You get to know the Lord as you pray daily. You talk to Him. You listen for His voice. And the more you hear His voice, the more discerning your ears become at recognizing Him.

GOD'S WILL—A PROCESS

As you grow in the Lord, responding in obedience to His guidance, the Father will entrust more and more to you: more responsibilities, more power, more authority, more blessings, more challenges. He knows He can share His heart's desire (His will) with you because you obey Him.

Bear in mind that maturing in the Lord is a process. No one steps, without fail, on every stepping stone. No one avoids every stumbling block, every time. It's a walk of faith. A relationship like this must be exercised and strengthened. It requires becoming acquainted with God and His ways.

When you stumble, get up! Ask God to forgive you. Commit yourself to getting back in the center of His will. Your life will never be the same.

A Final Word

STAYING IN GOD'S WILL

Trust in the Lord with all thine heart; and lean
not unto thine own understanding. In all thy
ways acknowledge him, and he shall direct thy
paths. (Prov. 3:5-6)

Twenty-five years after God called me to preach the Gospel,
our ministry in Orlando was bursting at the seams. Staff
members and volunteers were scattered across our ministry complex. After looking at the situation, it was obvious that
we had outgrown our property.

We were faced with the prospect of outsourcing parts of
our ministry and moving people to other facilities. I knew that
remaining in our then present location would stifle and perhaps
even halt our growth.

I prayed and asked God for direction, but none seemed to
come. Out of the blue, my wife, Suzanne, startled me by saying,
"Benny, the Lord spoke to me and said that the headquarters of
the healing ministry would move to Dallas, Texas."

"Dallas?" I responded in amazement. "Well, if God is really
talking to you, please tell the Lord to also speak to me." And then
the subject was dropped.

The next year, a similar experience took place. The Lord
spoke to me about moving our family to southern California,

where our television studio and media ministry had recently been relocated. When I shared this with Suzanne, she said, "Well, if this is important, the Lord will speak to both of us."

He did. By summer 1999, Suzanne and I both sensed a green light from God on both moves—to California and to Texas. When we discussed this with our board of directors, it kindled a burst of creativity and enthusiasm like none I had ever seen. During that meeting, the Holy Spirit refreshed and refined our vision to reach the world for Christ. It quickly became obvious to all of us that to accomplish what God had called us to do, this was the right decision.

Our accountants, after considerable analysis, agreed as well. "This is good stewardship," they told me. "Moving our headquarters to Dallas will save millions of dollars over the next few years."

Our family made the move to California. And we announced that the headquarters of the healing ministry was relocating to Dallas.

It's happened! Today, through the generous gifts of our partners we are together touching more hearts around the world than we ever imagined possible. Unbelievable doors of opportunity have opened in places formerly closed to ministry. From providing physical and spiritual food to children in the Philippines to building churches and orphanages in Mexico to holding international crusades and reaching around the globe with the Gospel through our daily *This Is Your Day!* telecasts, we are making an impact on our world for Jesus Christ.

Through its World Media Center, Benny Hinn Ministries and its partners are fulfilling the great commission of the Lord stated in Mark 16:15: "And he said unto them, Go ye into all the world, and preach the gospel to every creature."

It's taken many years for us to be able to discern God's will, even regarding such huge moves as the ones to Texas and California. The faith for the worldwide ministry we do today hasn't happened without challenges, detours, and learning how to walk in Him, one day at a time.

It's the same for each of us, no matter what we are called to do. It's a walk of faith that begins with small steps and then grows in direct proportion to our obedience to the Father's guidance.

THE WILL OF GOD

Every believer is called to hear God's voice and to follow His will. The key is keeping your heart pointed toward God. This is a lifelong endeavor and a constant challenge:

> And thou shall love the Lord thy God with all
> thine heart, and with all thy soul, and with all
> thy might. (Deut. 6:5)

Although knowing God's will is important, doing His will with a soft, pliable heart is the mark of true wisdom:

> And the world passeth away, and the lust
> thereof: but he that doeth the will of God
> abideth for ever. (1 John 2:17)

Our Father desires to spend time with us now as preparation for an eternity together with Him. He wants to be involved in everything we do. He desires to guide our steps. He cared enough to offer His only begotten Son's life as a sacrifice for the purpose of saving our souls and revealing His will to us.

No matter what's going on in your life right now, be encouraged. There is hope.

At the beginning of this book, I introduced you to Quan,

Betty, Mary, and Sam. Each had to make critical choices about the direction they wanted to go. Each is a Christian today. I wish I could report that each made the correct decisions, but it's simply not true in all four cases. Thank God for forgiveness and fresh tomorrows.

You see, most people know about God. Fewer know Him. Even fewer know and do His will. There is a big difference, and the choices we make are vital to the steps we take with Him. Quan, Betty, Mary, and Sam continue to learn these lessons, with varying degrees of success.

And for you, the question at this point is very simple: Are you willing to do whatever it takes to know God and to do the will of God? Are you willing to make your relationship with Him the most important part of your life? Are you willing to pay the price for such a wonderful walk with Him?

> I beseech you therefore, brethren, by the mercies of God, that ye present your bodies a living sacrifice, holy, acceptable unto God, which is your reasonable service. And be not conformed to this world: but be ye transformed by the renewing of your mind, that ye may prove what is that good, and acceptable, and perfect, will of God. (Rom. 12:1-2)

When Jesus prayed in the Garden of Gethsemane, even He came to the moment when, in the words of the powerful Bible teacher Matthew Henry, "He grounds his own willingness upon the Father's will." Jesus prayed:

> O my Father, if it be possible, let this cup pass from me: nevertheless not as I will, but as thou wilt. (Matt. 26:39)

I pray that the Holy Spirit will use this book to stir you to fulfill every desire that God has for your life. I pray that you will say with your whole heart, "Your will, Lord, not mine."